N T

O K

Making Meaning®

SECOND EDITION

Grade 1

Developmental Studies Center
2000 Embarcadero, Suite 305
Oakland, CA 94606-5300
(800) 666-7270, fax: (510) 464-3670
www.devstu.org

ISBN-13: 978-1-59892-702-3
ISBN-10: 1-59892-702-7

Printed in the United States of America

1 2 3 4 5 6 7 8 9 10 MLY 12 11 10 09 08

Table of Contents

Assessment Overview

The *Assessment Resource Book* is designed to help you record your observations and make informed instructional decisions as you teach the *Making Meaning®* lessons. The expectation in the *Making Meaning* program is that *all* of your students are developing at their own pace into readers with high levels of comprehension, and that they can all develop positive, effective interpersonal skills.

The assessment in *Making Meaning* grade 1 is a Class Progress Assessment (CPA), which is an informal once-a-week assessment designed to help you think about the performance and needs of the whole class. During a CPA, you have the opportunity to randomly observe students as they work in pairs or individually (selecting strong, average, and struggling readers) as you ask yourself key questions. Each week's CPA record sheet gives you space to record your observations.

As you follow the lessons in the *Teacher's Manual*, an assessment box will alert you whenever a CPA is suggested. The assessment box will also direct you to the corresponding page in the *Assessment Resource Book*.

IDR Conference Notes

Your notes from the IDR conferences you have with students are an important source of information about each student's development over time. Once your class begins Individualized Daily Reading (IDR) in Unit 4, it is important to document at least one conference per unit per student, using the "IDR Conference Notes" record sheet.

We suggest that you create individual student folders to collect each student's IDR conference notes, filed chronologically. This folder will comprise an informal portfolio that you can use to discuss the student's progress with the student or others.

Class Progress
Assessment

The Reading Life—Fiction and Narrative Nonfiction

Ask yourself:	Observation notes
▶ Are the students making connections to the story?	
▶ Are the students listening to each other?	
▶ What problems, if any, do I want to bring up at the end of the lesson?	

The Reading Life—Fiction and Narrative Nonfiction

Ask yourself:	Observation notes
▶ Do the students understand the surface level of the story? Are they able to follow the plot?	
▶ Are they able to connect their thinking to the text?	
▶ Are the students practicing the procedures for a read-aloud? What procedures do they have difficulty with?	
▶ How are they interacting and listening during "Turn to Your Partner"?	

Making Connections—Fiction

Ask yourself:	Observation notes
▶ Are the students making connections to important ideas or to details?	

Making Connections—Fiction

Ask yourself:	Observation notes
▶ Are both partners sharing their thinking?	
▶ Are they making connections to the part of the story they heard?	
▶ Are they connecting to the big ideas and feelings in that part of the story?	

Making Connections—Fiction

Ask yourself:	Observation notes
▶ *Are the students making connections to the part of the story they heard?*	
▶ *Are they connecting to the big ideas and feelings in that part of the story?*	

Retelling—Fiction

Ask yourself:	Observation notes
▶ Are the students referring to the text to retell the story?	
▶ Are they speaking so they can hear one another?	

Retelling—Fiction

Ask yourself:	Observation notes
▶ Are the students referring to the text to retell the story?	
▶ Are partners speaking so they can hear each other?	
▶ Do they help each other fill in gaps in the retelling?	

Retelling—Fiction

Ask yourself:	Observation notes
▶ Are the students able to sequence the events in the story?	
▶ Do they speak clearly when they share their thinking?	

Visualizing—Poetry and Fiction

Ask yourself:	Observation notes
▶ *Are the students' visualizations connected to words and phrases in the poem?*	

✐ **Visualizing**—Poetry and Fiction

Ask yourself:	Observation notes
▶ *Is there evidence in the students' drawings that they are thinking about the words in the text?*	

Visualizing—Poetry and Fiction

Ask yourself:	Observation notes
▶ *Do the students refer to the text as they describe their mental images?*	

Visualizing—Poetry and Fiction

Ask yourself:	Observation notes
▶ Are the students connecting their drawings to the story?	
▶ Are they using background knowledge to visualize the story?	

Wondering—Fiction and Narrative Nonfiction

Ask yourself:	Observation notes
▶ Are the students able to generate "I wonder" statements?	
▶ Are the statements relevant to the story?	

Wondering—Fiction and Narrative Nonfiction

Ask yourself:	Observation notes
▶ *Are the students able to generate "I wonder" statements?*	
▶ *Are the statements relevant to the story?*	

Wondering—Fiction and Narrative Nonfiction

Ask yourself:	Observation notes
▶ Do the students support their thinking by referring to the text?	
▶ Did the students generate a variety of "I wonder" statements?	

✎ **Making Connections**—Expository Nonfiction

Ask yourself:	Observation notes
▸ *Are the students able to make text-to-self connections?*	
▸ *Do the students easily share their ideas with their partners?*	

✏ **Making Connections**—Expository Nonfiction

Ask yourself:	Observation notes
▸ *Are the students able to remember the facts they hear?*	
▸ *Are the students able to make connections to the text?*	
▸ *Do the students listen carefully and share their ideas with their partners and the class?*	

Making Connections—Expository Nonfiction

Ask yourself:	Observation notes
▶ Are the students able to use schema to generate ideas that connect to the text?	
▶ Do the students listen carefully and share their ideas with their partners and the class?	

Wondering—Expository Nonfiction

Ask yourself:	Observation notes
▶ Are the students comprehending what they read?	
▶ Are they finding factual information?	

Wondering—Expository Nonfiction

Ask yourself:	Observation notes
▶ Are the students comprehending what they read?	
▶ Are they finding factual information?	

Wondering—Expository Nonfiction

Ask yourself:	Observation notes
▶ Are the students able to describe what they learn from the text?	
▶ Are their ideas connected to the text?	

✏️ **Exploring Text Features**—Expository Nonfiction

Ask yourself:	Observation notes
▶ *Do the students' labeled drawings show evidence that they understand the text?*	
▶ *Are they able to share their drawings in a caring and respectful way?*	

✎ **Exploring Text Features**—Expository Nonfiction

Ask yourself:	Observation notes
▶ *Do students' writings and discussions show evidence that they understand the text?*	
▶ *Do students' "wonderings" show evidence that they use the text to stimulate curiosity?*	
▶ *Are they beginning to use the features in their books to help them make sense of what they are reading?*	

Exploring Text Features—Expository Nonfiction

Ask yourself:	Observation notes
▶ Do students' discussions show evidence that they understand the text?	
▶ Do students' discussions show evidence that they are beginning to use text features?	
▶ Are students respectful and caring to each other as they share their findings?	

Blackline
Masters

Resource Sheet for IDR Conferences

General questions you can ask to probe student thinking:

▶ *Why did you choose this book?*

▶ *Why do you like/dislike this book?*

▶ *What kinds of books do you want to read?*

Genre-specific questions you can ask:

Fiction

▶ *What is this story about?*

▶ *What has happened so far?*

▶ *What do you know about the character(s)?*

▶ *What part have you found interesting or surprising? Why?*

▶ *What are you wondering about?*

▶ *What do you visualize (see/hear/feel) as you read these words?*

▶ *What do you think will happen next?*

Nonfiction/Expository

▶ *What is this [book/article] about?*

▶ (Read the information on the back cover.) *What have you found out about that so far?*

▶ (Look at the table of contents.) *What do you think you will find out about* _____ *in this book?*

▶ *What have you learned from reading this article?*

▶ *What's something interesting you've read so far?*

▶ *What are you wondering about?*

▶ *What do you expect to learn about as you continue to read?*

▶ *What information does this [diagram/table/graph/other text feature] give you?*

Poetry

▶ *What is this poem about?*

▶ *What do you visualize (see/hear/feel) as you read these words?*

▶ *What do you think the poet means by* _____ *?*

IDR Conference Notes

Student: _____ **Date:** _____

Book title: _____

EVIDENCE:

1 ▶ **Ask: What is your book about so far?**

Is the student able to describe the book?

YES

2 ▶ **Have the student read a passage silently, then read it aloud for you.**

Does the student:

	YES
Attend to meaning?	
Pause/reread if having difficulty?	
Read most words accurately?	
Try to make sense of unfamiliar language?	
Read fluently?	

3 ▶ **Ask: What is the part you just read about?**

Does the student recall what's important in the passage?

YES

If the student has difficulty, have him/her reread the passage and repeat Step ▶3.
If the student doesn't understand after the second reading, go to Step ▷4. *Otherwise, go to Step* ▶4.

4 ▷ **If the student doesn't understand after the second reading, ask yourself:**

Is the difficulty caused by:

Lack of background knowledge?	
Unfamiliar vocabulary?	
Too-difficult text (lack of fluency)?	
Not using an appropriate comprehension strategy?	

4 ▶ **Ask: What do you think will happen, or what do you think you will learn, as you keep reading?**

5 ▶ **Ask yourself: Is the student using comprehension strategies to make sense of text?**

5 ▷ **Intervene using one or more of the following:**

- Define unfamiliar words.
- Provide necessary background knowledge.
- Suggest an appropriate strategy on the "Reading Comprehension Strategies" chart and have the student reread again, starting at an earlier place in the text.
- Ask clarifying questions about the text.
- Help the student find a more appropriately leveled book.

Next steps:

Making Meaning® Reorder Information
SECOND EDITION

Kindergarten

Complete Classroom Package   **MM2-CPK**

Contents: Teacher's Manual, Orientation Handbook and DVDs, and 27 trade books

Available separately:

Classroom materials without trade books	MM2-TPK
Teacher's Manual	MM2-TMK
Trade book set (27 books)	MM2-TBSK

Grade 1

Complete Classroom Package   **MM2-CP1**

Contents: Teacher's Manual, Orientation Handbook and DVDs, Assessment Resource Book, and 28 trade books

Available separately:

Classroom materials without trade books	MM2-TP1
Teacher's Manual	MM2-TM1
Assessment Resource Book	MM2-AB1
Trade book set (28 books)	MM2-TBS1

Grade 2

Complete Classroom Package   **MM2-CP2**

Contents: Teacher's Manual, Orientation Handbook and DVDs, class set (25 Student Response Books, Assessment Resource Book), and 29 trade books

Available separately:

Classroom materials without trade books	MM2-TP2
Teacher's Manual	MM2-TM2
Replacement class set	MM2-RCS2
CD-ROM Grade 2 Reproducible Materials*	MM2-CDR2
Trade book set (29 books)	MM2-TBS2

Grade 3

Complete Classroom Package   **MM2-CP3**

Contents: Teacher's Manual (2 volumes), Orientation Handbook and DVDs, class set (25 Student Response Books, Assessment Resource Book), and 26 trade books

Available separately:

Classroom materials without trade books	MM2-TP3
Teacher's Manual, vol. 1	MM2-TM3-V1
Teacher's Manual, vol. 2	MM2-TM3-V2
Replacement class set	MM2-RCS3
CD-ROM Grade 3 Reproducible Materials*	MM2-CDR3
Trade book set (26 books)	MM2-TBS3

Grade 4

Complete Classroom Package   **MM2-CP4**

Contents: Teacher's Manual (2 volumes), Orientation Handbook and DVDs, class set (30 Student Response Books, Assessment Resource Book), and 24 trade books

Available separately:

Classroom materials without trade books	MM2-TP4
Teacher's Manual, vol. 1	MM2-TM4-V1
Teacher's Manual, vol. 2	MM2-TM4-V2
Replacement class set	MM2-RCS4
CD-ROM Grade 4 Reproducible Materials*	MM2-CDR4
Trade book set (24 books)	MM2-TBS4

Grade 5

Complete Classroom Package   **MM2-CP5**

Contents: Teacher's Manual (2 volumes), Orientation Handbook and DVDs, class set (30 Student Response Books, Assessment Resource Book), and 19 trade books

Available separately:

Classroom materials without trade books	MM2-TP5
Teacher's Manual, vol. 1	MM2-TM5-V1
Teacher's Manual, vol. 2	MM2-TM5-V2
Replacement class set	MM2-RCS5
CD-ROM Grade 5 Reproducible Materials*	MM2-CDR5
Trade book set (19 books)	MM2-TBS5

Grade 6

Complete Classroom Package   **MM2-CP6**

Contents: Teacher's Manual (2 volumes), Orientation Handbook and DVDs, class set (30 Student Response Books, Assessment Resource Book), and 19 trade books

Available separately:

Classroom materials without trade books	MM2-TP6
Teacher's Manual, vol. 1	MM2-TM6-V1
Teacher's Manual, vol. 2	MM2-TM6-V2
Replacement class set	MM2-RCS5
CD-ROM Grade 6 Reproducible Materials*	MM2-CDR6
Trade book set (19 books)	MM2-TBS6

Ordering Information:

To order call 800.666.7270 * fax 510.842.0348
log on to www.devstu.org * e-mail pubs@devstu.org

Or Mail Your Order to:

Developmental Studies Center * Publications Department
2000 Embarcadero, Suite 305 * Oakland, CA 94606-5300

* CD-ROMs available Summer 2009

DEVELOPMENTAL STUDIES CENTER™